JULIE DAVIDSON has had a long, varied and award-winning career in Scottish and UK journalism. She began her training with D.C. Thomson, where she edited romantic fiction and composed – i.e. invented – the horoscopes for *Secrets* magazine. After a spell on the *Aberdeen Press and Journal* she became a staff feature writer and columnist on *The Scotsman*, then a columnist and critic on *The Glasgow Herald*, for whom she won five Scottish Press Awards. She has also contributed to *The Times*, *The Observer*, *The Guardian*, *The Daily Telegraph*, *Cosmopolitan* and *House and Garden*, and was a presenter of *What the Papers Say* during the golden years of Granada Television. In the past 10 years she has concentrated mainly on travel writing (for which she has won Scottish, UK and Canadian awards). She is currently researching a book on Mary Livingstone, wife of Scotland's iconic missionary-explorer.

BOB DEWAR was born in Edinburgh at an early age, 16 years later he was published nationally. He worked in D.C. Thomson's studio where, among other things, he ghosted Dennis the Menace. After going freelance, he did political and social commentary for *The Scotsman* newspaper. He has illustrated books for the children's and English Speaking Departments of Oxford University Press, Fife Educational

Social Development, A&C Black and most Scottish publishers –
Birlinn, Luath, Black & White and Itchy Coo. His work has also
appeared in *The Times*, *The Herald*, *Scottish Field* and The
Scotch Malt Whisky Society. He has had exhibitions in Lucca,
Italy, Glasgow and Edinburgh and had caricatures hanging in
the House of Commons. He is now a lot older than 16 and is
married to the novelist Isla Dewar, with two sons and an
absurdly friendly big golden retriever. He has no idea how this
friendliness happened, since he tends toward grumpiness.

SCOTS WE KEN

Words by JULIE DAVIDSON

Illustrations by BOB DEWAR

Luath Press Limited

EDINBURGH

www.luath.co.uk

First Published 2007

ISBN (10) 1 906307 008
ISBN (13) 978-1-906307-00-4

The paper used in this book is recyclable. It is made from
low chlorine pulps produced in a low energy, low emission
manner from renewable forests.

Printed and bound by Grafo, Bilbao

Typeset in 11pt Century Schoolbook by 3btype.com

To my best friends: Harry Reid, my husband,
and Catherine Reid, my daughter.
With love and thanks for keeping me right on sport,
whisky and undergraduate style.

CONTENTS

8

INTRODUCTION

There is one kenspeckle character conspicuous by his – or
her – absence in this light-hearted gallery of familiar faces:
The Veteran Hack. I might have used myself and some of my
best friends as a composite model, and maybe I'll do so yet in a
future collection. But at the moment the morale of the Scottish
media, in print and broadcast journalism, is almost beyond a
joke. The talent and commitment of Scottish journalists have
not diminished, but at a time when they should be most
inspired by the shifting tectonic plates in Scotland's political
status their work and influence have been undermined by lack
of resources, enfeebled managements and, in some cases,
uninterested and remote proprietors for whom our resurgent
nation means nothing but a source of profit.

Why introduce a book which is essentially a caper
– a bit of mischief at the expense of our ambivalent view of
ourselves – with a lament? Partly because I've spent 40 years
working in the Scottish media, and am dismayed by the wounded
vitality of our once-great newspapers and semi-detached news
organisations at a time when their energy is most needed; but
also because *Scots We Ken*, which is predicated on the notion
that the cultural nuances of our Scottishness inform a range of

social types, is a minor piece of evidence that the indigenous publishing industry is in buoyant form; and draws strength, along with our domestic theatre, music and art, from a sense that the optimism and opportunities which arrived in 1999 with Scotland's re-instated Parliament have refreshed and invigorated our cultural life.

A resurgent Scotland should mean a resurgent media. Perhaps it is time for some cross-party parliamentary thinking on what can be done to safeguard the future of the indigenous Scottish Press. Action has already been taken on the future of broadcasting.

Scots We Ken owes its genesis to one enduring publication: the monthly magazine *Scottish Field*, which was founded in 1903 and has had a new lease of life under its present owners, *Oban Times Ltd*. I'm indebted to its former editor, Claire Grant, who came up with the concept and commissioned the perfect illustrator, Bob Dewar, to interpret the text, put exuberant flesh on my fantasy figures and add his own wicked details. During the run-up to the 1979 devolution referendum, when I was working for *The Scotsman*, I was one of a team of writers who collaborated with Bob on a cartoon series called The Devolvers. That referendum, of course, didn't deliver. Thirty years on it's thus especially satisfying to work again with one of Scotland's finest satirical artists in an effectively devolved Scotland. I'd also like to thank those friends – you know who you are – whose brains I picked for information on the current temperaments of Munrobaggers, members of the National Trust for Scotland and captains of posh golf clubs.

Under the title Scots Cornered the series ran for almost two years in *Scottish Field*, which is why there is a rural bias in many of the profiles, but I have tried to redress the balance by adding three new urban types: The Football Supporter, The Ex-Pat and The Last Publican. I'm also conscious that there is a middle-class bias in the medley, causing serious gaps in this pantheon of iconic personalities. Where is The Ned, for example? Or The Big Issue Seller? Or The Demotic Writer? They will not be neglected in any future series of Scots We Ken.

Despite their absence it's my hope that many Scots, with a wry smile, will recognise and own up to little bits of themselves in the men and women in these pages. Even me. There is, for example, something unnervingly familiar about the Lady Who Lunches… and don't I know that woman driver who ignores the Parent and Child signs on parking spaces?

Julie Davidson,
Edinburgh, 2007

As soon as Hamish St John Nevis hears the crunch of tyres on
the gravel he picks up the sgian-dhub from his desk, where it
doubles as paper knife, slides it **THE HIGHLAND HOTELIER**
into his stocking, calls the red setters to heel and marches to
the front door. 'Welcome! I'm Captain St John Nevis, the
Meeter and Greeter.' He gives a knowing, ironic laugh, inviting
complicity in this vulgarism. 'Welcome to Tigh a' Mamore!
My better half is in the kitchen, as ever, but there's a wee glass
of sherry waiting for you in your room.'

Hamish dreams of receiving guests who drive Bentleys
or Aston Martins; not so much because these vehicles signify
affluence but because they are rare survivors of the British
marque – standard-bearers of a golden age of quality car
production. In the competitive world of upmarket tourism,
however, he has to take what he gets: Americans in hired
Hondas, the French in their own Renaults, the Swedes in their
own Volvos and the British in anything from Tyne-built
Nissans to imported Mazdas.

The new arrivals are thirty-somethings who have parked
their BMW with its nearside wheels on the lawn. 'Sorry to be a
fusspot, but do you mind re-parking? The poor old turf will turn
to mud if you leave it there.' Either honeymooners or adulterers,
he judges. Best keep them away from Betsy, who gets snappy
in the presence of public romancing.

'Now, house rules,' he says, showing them up the walnut staircase. 'There are none! We like our guests to feel they're staying with old friends, so we'll expect you for cocktails at seven. You *will* be in for dinner, won't you? We need to know now so Mrs St John Nevis can get her act together. Oh yes – jacket in the dining room and no jeans. You can do away with the old school tie, if you like! Got to keep up with the times.'

Jamie and Sarah, who have been married for six years and seldom escape from their work stations in the City, glance at each other. Jamie has packed only jeans and joggers, and after the long drive from London they are looking forward to a quiet meal and an early night. 'Is there anywhere else to eat near here?'

Hamish looks at him sharply. 'The Clansman in the village does pub suppers. We have four stars in the Gourmet Guide, you know. All our produce is locally sourced, we have a splendid chap who dives for our scallops, the venison comes off the hill and the veg is all organic. See you at seven.'

By 7.15 three other couples and a lone fisher are standing with their drinks in the handsome hall. Betsy has appeared briefly to receive their compliments for the canapés – miniature black puddings on tiny oatcakes, smoked oysters in nests of samphire – and Hamish is explaining, 'The previous owners called it Mamore Hotel, but we thought that sounded a bit commercial. 'Tigh' means 'house' in Gaelic, much more our kind of thing. Suits the house party ambience.'

'Do you speak Gaelic?' asks Sarah, who is trying to compensate for Jamie's jeans. Hamish twinkles at her. 'Not as such. I'm Scottish, of course, but I was born in Swindon. Didn't come north until I joined the Argylls. But I do know the meaning of Mamore. 'Mam' is Gaelic for breast, often used for hills. And 'more' means big. So this is the House of the Big Breast. Ha!'

Jamie also says 'Ha!' when he studies their bill the next morning. 'Old friends? What kind of old friends charge you £305.70 for dinner, bed and breakfast?'

A social encounter during Tartan Week in New York finally
convinces Karen it is time to return to the Best Small Country
in the World. After nine years selling real estate in Houston, a
bare-knuckle divorce suit and four years of internet dating in
Manhattan she feels she is can-done with the can-do culture of
America. When she is introduced over promotional
cocktails to the marketing director of Gay Granite, a company
which salvages Rubislaw stone from condemned buildings and
turns it into kitchen worktops, her eyes turn misty.

THE EX-PAT

His Buchan banter fills her with nostalgia, his retro-
kilt exposes knees like tumshies ('authentic clan tartan – ye
winna catch me in fashion fabrics like wee Jackie McConnell')
and his expense account accommodates dinner for two at
L'Atelier de Joel Robuchon in the Four Seasons. 'With your
experience,' he enthuses, 'ye could clean up back home. They
can't build houses fast enough in Edinburgh, every high street
in Scotland is thick with estate agents and even my personal
trainer has seven letting properties.'

Five months and one job interview later Karen is home.
Not to pursue romance (the marketing director, she has learned,
is as solidly gay as his product) but to buy into Edinburgh's
Docklands with the lump sum from her divorce settlement.
'Scotland has discovered the penthouse duplex with wraparound

terrace!' she merrily informs her New York friend Emily. 'For five hundred grand – pounds, of course – I can almost imagine the Forth is the East River.' Emily, who struggles to rent a Tribeca shoebox with views of a stairwell, promises to visit.

Karen's mother is less impressed. 'It's a lot to pay for a flat,' she opines. 'You could have bought a nice bungalow in Corstorphine for that money, with a bit of garden to sit in. Have you not had your fill of skyscrapers? After all, you're not getting any younger and a garden is a great comfort to a single woman.' (She has never quite forgiven Karen for divorcing the exotic Aaron, a 'real Southern gent' who called her Momma Scotch, plied her with Margaritas and, on her Houston visits, funded several treatments of lip-plumping and skin-peeling at a highly reputable beauty parlour.)

Delighted with her new home, Karen finds her new job disappointing. The partners are Old Fettesians who specialise in country estates. They have hired her to build up a prestige portfolio of urban mansions and townhouses, but give her little guidance and spend much of their time out of the office lunching threadbare lairds, or 'making a day of it' in Argyll and Perthshire. She has not missed their condescending smiles when, with a slip of the tongue, she calls herself a 'realtor', and she discovers her hybrid accent does her telephone manner no

20

favours. 'Everyone seems to think I'm cold-calling from Bangalore,' she complains.

Edinburgh, where she went to college 17 years ago, confuses her. She reports to Emily: 'It's the biggest financial centre outside London, there are lots of flash new eating places and style bars, but they still can't think outside the box. I can't find anywhere which does dinner after 10pm and there's no such thing as a 24-hour bookshop.'

Karen has ambition. The langourous practices of the Old Fettesians soon frustrate her, but when she takes her own business plan to a merchant banker – 'I think I can bring some US dynamism to the property market' – she finds the venture capitalist unadventurous. 'I'm not sure,' he muses, 'that the hard sell goes down well in Scotland.'

She sends a despairing email to Emily: 'Best Small Country in the World? Only if you never leave it.'

Throughout his long career Russell Clapshot has held to the belief that 'thinking time' is critical to the political process. When he was in local government (deputy convener until he resigned over a PFI initiative on adventure playgrounds) he used his rural commute to sort out his ideas; during his brief time at Westminster the Thursday sleeper from King's Cross was an aid to contemplation; and when he made the decision to embrace Europe ('better on the inside spitting out than the outside spitting in') he discovered the value of post-prandial reflection.

THE MSP

Russell sometimes thinks wistfully of those stupendous Brussels lunches in Michelin-rated restaurants off the Grand Place; gossiping waspishly with colleagues, giving off-the-record briefings to the European editors of the Scottish dailies. Now the European editors have been repatriated; the political forces of the Fourth Estate are embedded in Holyrood, where they spend much time grumbling about their reduced expenses and cadging drinks off the more gullible MSPs.

In the twilight of his political life, however, Holyrood represents sheltered housing to Russell. He still contributes vigorously to debates and aspires to serve on committees, but his ambition has lost its edge. He feels comfortable in the great granite and oak monument to Donald Dewar and Enrico

RODIN'S
DRINKER

Miralles, where there is little risk of being patronised by Old Etonians or confused by Walloons. True, Russell voted against increasing the budget to meet the building's costs, but now he takes pleasure in guiding groups of constituents round the Scottish Parliament, and is particularly delighted to show them his Pod.

'Specially designed for The Thinker!' He demonstrates by planking his substantial bottom (a legacy of Brussels) on the seat in the elegant window recess of his office, leans his elbow on his knee and puts his fist to his forehead in tribute to the famous Rodin statue. His audience gives uncertain giggles, and at the other end of the office his secretary rolls her eyes. She has seen this performance many times; she has a mountain of correspondence waiting for Russell's attention; and she has set her heart on attending the Festival of Politics drinks reception in the Garden Lobby. 'Get them out of here before they smell the booze,' she urges silently.

Kenspeckle veterans like Russell are fixtures on Holyrood's party invitation lists. Non-parliamentary guests are reassured by his familiar face, and although they struggle to remember his constituency they associate his prodigious sideburns and bow ties with political celebrity. The invitees, who might include captains of Scotland's service industries, newspaper editors, NGO directors and – barely concealing their condescending smirks – the occasional Westminster MP, have been known to remark over-loudly, 'Who are all these people?' Which has the undesirable effect of drawing attention to the invisible status of most MSPs.

Russell, however, has no difficulty in drawing attention to himself at Holyrood parties. He has the deft ability to lift four glasses of wine at once from the speeding trays of waiters, thus guaranteeing his place amid a cluster of guests, although his conviviality is not without hazard. Once he found himself addressing a female guest on the need to strengthen the powers of the devolved parliament. As he moved on to the subject of wind farms, capturing another two drinks from a passing waiter, he mistook the glassy look in her eyes for rapt attention.

'Would you like to see one of the famous Pods?' he twinkled. 'My office is just down the corridor.'

The young woman gave him a fierce stare. 'I've got my own Pod, thanks very much,' she snapped. 'I've been a Member here since 2002.'

Senga is fuming. It is ten past three in Annie Laurie's Surf and Turf Bistro and there are four lunch customers who show no sign of leaving. They ordered their third bottle of wine with another round of coffees just before the kitchen closed, and Senga has a hair appointment at Prime Cuts in Ayr. She needs her roots done, but she also needs to be back on duty by 6.30.

'Ah'll miss ma bus if they toffs dinny get their bee-tees oota here,' she complains to Elena, who has recently arrived from Krakow and, despite competent English, finds Senga's conversation mystifying. 'Nae consideration fur workin' mothers.'

The young waitress looks even more bemused. Senga's children, she knows, have long since left home. Michelle works in quality control in an East Kilbride supermarket and Wayne is a mobile phone salesman in Glasgow. They each live with their respective partners – a word their mother treats with suspicion. 'Partners? Whit kind o' business are they runnin'? In ma day it was called a bidie-in, and it wis naethin' tae be proud o'.'

Senga is proud of her children, nonetheless, especially when they call their jobs 'a promising career path'. She has been a waitress all her working life and the only career path she has known is the route from kitchen to table. Things might have been different if she and Willie had stayed in Glasgow,

THE NIPPY SWEETIE

where her most fulfilling years were spent in the dining room of the Royal Scottish Automobile Club in Blythswood Square. 'A decent class o' customer who expected decent standards,' she tells Elena. 'Silver service. Port with the Stilton. And aye the time to huv a wee joke with their favourite waitress.'

By the time the family moved to Ayr the hospitality industry was changing and Senga knew her days were numbered. The posher dining rooms of the Ayrshire coast had maître d's who had been to hotel school and seasonal staff who arrived in Scotland by way of Bali, Goa, and the Greek islands: bright young Aussies and Kiwis on gap years with waiting skills restricted to willing smiles and inexhaustible energy. 'And they've nae idea whit broon sauce is fur.'

Her job at Annie Laurie's, she reckons, will be her last. The wayside eatery would have been called a 'roadhouse' in the 1950s and is less dependent on seasonal staff than the seaside hotels. The management value Senga's experience and respect tradition, providing her with a black dress, white pinny and starched cap – the uniform she has always worn. She once walked out of a so-called 'style bar' where the waitress had a nose ring and three inches of bare flesh overhanging her jeans. 'Ah telt her ah didnae want to gaze inty her navel when Ah was orderin' ma Buffalo Wings.'

But the future is Elena, and Marik from Vilnius who does the wine. The gap year students come and go, but the Poles and Lithuanians are here to stay. And Senga is forced to admit they're good workers. 'Ye've a lot tae learn, a' the same,' she says, having lost patience with the party who have outstayed their welcome. 'Here's how ye get rid o' customers who huv nae respect for ither folks' time.'

She retreats briefly to the still room and re-emerges with a vacuum cleaner. When it starts to roar the foursome look irritated, but tough it out until Senga reaches their table, bangs the machine against their chairs and bellows above the noise, 'Wid ye mind shiftin' yer feet? Ah canny get away afore Ah've done the hooverin'.'

Like the carpet, they know when they're beaten.

By the time he was 15 Gavin was quite the bibliophile. His rural high school pointed him in the direction of Angus Wilson and Lawrence Durrell, but was slightly more sniffy about his precocious interest in Henry Miller. When Gavin discovered that all three literary giants were to take part in an international writers' conference at the Edinburgh Festival he persuaded his parents to fund a visit to Auntie Morag in Comely Bank. And so he found himself, on a summer day in 1962, in the McEwan Hall, witness to an occasion which still glows in his memory.

'Filth on the Fringe!' was the *Daily Express*'s critique of the moment when the writers' conference (to illustrate some long-forgotten creative point) startled its audience with an unscheduled piece of performance art. The nude model, pushed in a wheelbarrow across the gallery, was THE FESTIVAL FANS the first naked woman Gavin had ever seen. 'Hard to imagine the impact,' he tells Stephanie dreamily, although she has heard his account of *The Happening* many times before. 'These days it's more shocking if people keep their kit ON.'

Gavin prides himself on his command of contemporary idiom, which he has acquired over many August evenings spent at The Stand and the Gilded Balloon. Since his children grew up and his wife ran off with her life coach he has been

1962

able to re-visit his passion for Edinburgh's carnival of culture on annual holidays. The monstrous growth of the Fringe excites him, and when the Book Festival first opened his cup ranneth over. He has now found a mid-life partner who shares his eclectic tastes ('We're up for anything from James MacMillan to the Bangkok Ladyboys!') and they are famous for their methodical planning and formidable stamina.

As soon as all four programmes are released – Steph is something of a cineaste, so they don't ignore the Film Festival – they book their selected highlights on-line, but leave scope for spontaneity. 'Too much forward planning dulls the appetite for experiment,' insists Gavin. Off comes his city suit (he is now a hospital administrator in Paddington) and on go his summer jacket of unstructured linen and elderly jeans. Off come Stephanie's mumsy prints (she teaches English to civil servants from Slovenia) and on go her cheesecloth blouse and ankle-length Kurdish skirt. They keep their footwear sturdy: trekkers or all-terrain sandals, and carry their water bottles and programmes in little Rajasthani rucksacks sparkling with mirrors.

They take a lofty view of their accommodation needs, preferring to devote their budget to the arts. For the past seven years they have stayed in the same vegetarian guest house in Polmont. Their landlady, Deirdre, is a practising Buddhist and

ex-dancer who performed briefly with the Nederlands Dans
Theatre, and through her cultural network Gavin and Steph
are sometimes admitted to the social circuit of receptions and
awards ceremonies. Over Bucks Fizz and croissants they have
applauded winners of the Herald Angels, they were given
complimentary seats for the gala premier of Wong Kar-Wai's
In the Mood for Love and – most thrillingly – they were once
invited to a private party thrown by Ricky Demarco.

Each year they delight in breaking their own record as
the festival city's most diligent consumers. Eight events per
day is their current average but this year, by some catastrophic
miscalculation, they find themselves short of somewhere to go
on their last night. 'Nothing else for it,' says Gavin gloomily.
He is more of an elitist than he likes to think. 'We'll just have
to go and stand in Princes Street for the Fireworks Concert.'

Seona was born on 12 May 1983, the day after Aberdeen won the European Cup-Winners' Cup. She arrived a week early, and her mother has never quite forgiven her father for missing her birth. But Seona believes he made the only possible choice, given the clash of fixtures. She has grown up with the framed photograph of Dad and Uncle Harry waving from the deck of the St Clare, the chartered ferry which carried supporters across the North Sea to the final against Real Madrid in Gothenburg; and she never tires of his account of the game's climactic moment – the winning goal from super-sub John Hewitt in extra time – and the triumphant voyage home. 'Four hundred delirious fans on one ship and not a light bulb broken.'

Uncle Harry bought her a Dons strip for her fourth birthday and her father took her to her first match at Pittodrie when she was six. She has never forgotten the impact of that mighty space, brilliant with colour and surging with noise. The scarlet and blue spectacle (the Dons were playing Rangers) and the behaviour of the **THE FOOTBALL SUPPORTER** crowd, mainly adults and 'big boys', startled and awed her. She had never seen grown-ups behaving so oddly, so intensely uninhibited, and for the next few years she was less fascinated by the drama on the field than the drama on the terraces: the licensed yobbery, the curses and roars, the liberal deployment of the very worst 'sweary words'.

Until she was eight her father was able to persuade her that 'useless currant' was an innocuous insult, and could be legitimately directed at blind referees and inept goalkeepers. By the time street wisdom kicked in she had transferred her attention to the game, could recite the names of the 1983 cup-winning team, identify every player in the current squad and analyse the run of play. As a 10-year-old she would remark sagely, 'They're losing it in midfield.' Throughout her teens, when Aberdeen languished near the bottom of the Premier league, she kept her faith with her season ticket. 'I'm not just a glory-hunter,' she would tell uncomprehending friends, for whom dreich, dour, dismal winter afternoons and persistent failure seemed equally tormenting. 'The Dons need my support even more when they're down.'

Managers – or 'coaches' as Seona calls them – came and went. A signed photograph of Alex Ferguson, architect of the Dons' golden years but now a world figure at Manchester United, followed her from home to university to Perth, and the flat she now shares with an unemployed beauty therapist who is 'holding out' for a job at Gleneagles. Seona has sought work in Perth to be perfectly positioned to attend every home and away match played by Aberdeen.

She has not yet settled into a career worthy of her

degree in Sports Science, and is a lifeguard at the local swimcentre. Here she meets Charlie, a fellow lifeguard, and falls in love. Charlie is saving for a round-the-world air ticket and his Big Trip, which has a tick-list of global wonders from Angkor Wat to Easter Island, and proposes that Seona joins him on the Inca Trail to Machu Picchu. 'I'm aiming to be in Peru by September,' he tells her. 'So you'd better come out for the whole month.'

Seona agonises. A recent upturn in Aberdeen's fortunes has seen them qualify for Europe for the first time since she was born. September will mark the start of their journey to possible victory in the UEFA Cup.

There is no real choice, given the clash of fixtures. Lovers come and go. But a football team is for life.

Fingal's real name is Fred. His father was a Cockney haberdasher who left the rat race before the rats started running, relocating from Whitechapel to Inverness in 1959. The Highland capital was his wife's birthplace, and the couple opened a gift shop called Nessie's Nest near the canal. At primary school Fred was introduced to the Gay Gordons and The Dashing White Sergeant, and at the age of 11 he was taken to his first ceilidh, in a licensed hall on the Black Isle.

After a pint or three, nothing stops him recalling the life-changing events of that long ago night: 'I was flung off my feet by a lassie with a beehive as big as the real thing, I ate three platefuls of stovies, and I cadged my first dram off a drunk ferryman at the bar. But it was the Box which made my head reel. I'll never forget the lad on the accordion, his fingers dancin', the jaunty look o' him, and all the girls after a squeeze o' his Box.'

Fred formed his first band when he was 18. He had enough respect for his father to retain his East End surname (Mitchell) for everyday use, but on stage he was Fingal McCool, Genie of the Box, the creative force behind the Boys o' the Bothy. With Aly on drums, Phil on **THE CEILIDH BAND LEADER** fiddle and Robin MacGregor on acoustic guitar they were much in demand on the village dance circuit of the Eastern

Highlands and the Moray Firth. Fingal even began to believe it would soon be possible to give up his day job.

Nessie's Nest was expanding with the tourist industry, and Fingal was its head buyer: diligent at sourcing clan badges, ceramic stags, toy bagpipes, pictorial calendars (he takes some of the credit for promoting the romantic landscape photographer Calum Bailie) tartan ties, Saltire tee-shirts and the widest range of cuddly Monsters north of Fort William. But his heart was in show business; the band was seldom out of weekend work, got the odd spot on Radio Highland and just failed to secure a record deal.

Loyal to his Boys o' the Bothy, Fingal turned down the chance to perform a duet with Jimmy Shand on the White Heather Club. But the Boys were to prove less faithful to him. The world of Scottish popular music was changing. Radical influences were redefining traditional airs, country dance tunes, and Gaelic ballads of unrequited love and death by drowning. In the early 70s Robin left to pursue a career in contemporary folk, and had some success with his first composition, *A Hard Wind is A-Blowin' Us to Hell*, although his enigmatic follow-up, *Lassie in the Sea with Sapphires*, flopped. Phil joined a Gaelic rock group, and after emigrating to Kentucky Aly founded the tribute band Capercaillie Clones.

Only Fingal has remained true to his early calling, adding Calling to his repertoire. His re-constituted Scottish country dance band is now a ceilidh band, and Fingal calls dance directions to sweating and confused tourists at coach party hotels. He is not too proud to be the warm-up band at weddings, although he stoops now over his Box and his fingers are stiffer. He retreats to the bar when the DJ takes over, but his face wears a gentle smile. When the bridal couple takes the floor he knows he can still tug the heartstrings with his elegiac version of the Eriskay Love Lilt. 'Ye're aye the real thing, Fingal,' says the bride's father, buying him a large malt. 'Whaur's yer Runrig noo?'

When Derek was relocated to Aberdeen from Paris he had mixed feelings, but Louise was jubilant. Five years in the French capital were five years **THE COUNTRY COMMUTER** too many in her opinion; she had been more comfortable in Houston, Texas, where at least she spoke the language and the locals enjoyed telling her that seven 'Scotchmen' had fallen at the Battle of the Alamo. The Parisians looked blank if she mentioned the Auld Alliance.

Louise spent part of her childhood in Aberdeen, in the days when the benisons of the North Sea were limited to fish and family holidays. Her memories are filtered through a prism unsmeared by any trace of oil: bike rides to the Loch of Skene, picnics in the Forest of Birse, boisterous summer games (keeping warm was a factor) among the sand dunes of Balmedie. 'The Dee valley!' she enthuses to Derek, 'If we live in the country the girls can have riding lessons at last.'

Derek is an urban animal but a good parent. He can see the advantages for his family: clean air, little traffic, rural schools, a neighbourly environment where everyone looks out for each other. And so they buy a converted mill five miles from Banchory, the Deeside town, which, in Louise's absence, has become a busy hub of the Aberdeen commute.

'Used to be fields and woods up here,' she muses, as

they make their way to their new home through Banchory's suburbia – Cala villas, double garages, ambitious conservatories, expansive decks. But the mill is sufficiently remote to fulfil Louise's dreams, the girls are enchanted with the black-and-white waterwheel feature ('Not the original, I'm afraid,' she tells friends, 'it was too far gone to save.') and their nearest neighbours are farmers.

It is late summer when they arrive. Kirsty and Megan have been enrolled in the local primary school 'for the time being,' and Derek's first task is to buy a second car. Louise proposes a Range Rover – the lane to the mill will be tricky in winter – but her husband insists they can only afford a Toyota Rava. 'The Peugeot gobbles fuel hammering in and out to Aberdeen every day.'

He has been cast down by his first journeys. The quiet country roads of Louise's memory are now restless arteries prone to sclerosis at each commuter village. The mill is only 23 miles out of town, but he takes 90 minutes to reach Bridge of Don at peak times and has started staying late at the office to beat the evening exodus. In Paris he was often home in time to help with homework. 'La Defense to Neuilly, 10 minutes on the Metro,' he tells his new colleagues.

Louise finds that she too spends a lot of time in the car.

44

There is the school run, a return trip of 10 miles, and although she tries to combine it with food shopping she hasn't yet mastered the rural craft of bulk buying. Her years in Paris have compromised her ability to forward plan. There, if she forgot something, the charcuterie was just round the corner; here she finds herself driving to Banchory at least twice a day to track down artichokes or Arborio rice.

A priority is the girls' riding lessons, and to seek information Louise visits the farm. It is not what she expects; no clucking chickens or lowing Aberdeen Angus, but a silent yard and a putrid smell. 'That's the fertiliser,' says Mrs Buchan, who is cautiously friendly. 'We're arable here.' Louise isn't sure what arable means, but rushes on with her inquiry.

'Riding stables?' The farmer's wife ponders. 'Your best bet is Aberdeen.'

When he first took up golf Innes Oliver was apprenticed to an
eminent firm of solicitors, and believed that his dealings with
the Law would be confined to conveyancing and executry. But
over the years – he is now the senior partner and has become
captain of the golf club which accepted his membership four
decades ago – his sport has **THE GOLF CLUB CAPTAIN**
come under pressure from a climate created by meddlesome
pieces of legislation, usually involving women and religious
minorities. 'Not that it was ever true we blocked applications
from Jews and Catholics,' he tells Graham, the new steward.
'But rumours like these are bad for the game's image.'

Innes is not an unreasonable man. As captain of
Pinkie Links he does his best to defend tradition while
persuading members to accept the compromises of changing
times. Some years ago the dress code was relaxed to permit the
wearing of shorts in summer weather – as long as they were
'tailored shorts worn with three-quarters hose'. There are
limits, of course. 'Shirts must have collars' is the rule book's
slippery regulation for outlawing tee-shirts, while jeans are
also proscribed.

The influence of America has also had its impact.
Some recent anguish was caused when a foursome of young
members took to wearing their golf caps back to front. Despite

his high office and low handicap Innes dislikes confrontation, and chose to ask Graham to have a quiet word with the offenders in the Dirty Bar. 'You might also mention,' he added, 'that Sir Hector saw one of them grounding his iron in a bunker.'

If the etiquette of the game is increasingly beleaguered by the oafishness of modern life, Innes does recognise that attitudes to women require reform. Although Pinkie Links continues to deny them membership the club now allows the ladies to play as their husbands' guests. 'We've even installed a ladies' loo in a Portacabin at the ninth hole,' he proudly tells visitors. 'And we've reserved the rear porch of the clubhouse for their exclusive use. The junior barman pops through now and then to take drinks orders.'

On a fine summer morning, wearing his favourite Pringle sweater and an old tweed cap, there is nothing Innes enjoys more than a peaceful perambulation around the boundaries of his fiefdom: the larks rising from the rough; the pristine sand of the bunkers; the sound of the sea beyond the dunes; and, above all, the tender turf of the fairways and greens. He even smiles benignly on the young foursome in their properly adjusted Nike caps and – what do they call them? – 'cargo' trousers.

Suddenly his reverie is interrupted by the appearance

of two figures emerging from the woods. They are wearing hefty boots and carrying walking poles, and at their side is a prancing Labrador. Disbelievingly he watches them set off across the fairway towards the beach, their sticks flicking the turf and – his eyes bulge – their dog lifting its leg against the flagpole of the 16th hole.

Mild, non-confrontational Innes is stung into action. 'You people!' He roars, chasing after them. 'This is a golf course! Private Property! You've no right to be here unless you're members of Pinkie Links!'

The couple pause, turn and give him a knowing smile. 'We have every right to be here. Haven't you heard of the Land Reform Act, 2003? The Right to Roam?'

Innes falls back, flummoxed. Even the Law, to which he has dedicated his professional life, is encouraging the barbarians to breach the gates.

The Manse is a kit house beside the filling station on the edge of the village. It does have a sea view (pity about the fish farm) but when Bethany first applied for the vacancy at the linked parishes of Glenpibroch, Dunmachar and Nocht she imagined a different home: Victorian, perhaps, with white-washed harling, bay windows and a mature garden protected by shrubs. The Manse garden – a draughty square of decommissioned grazing land – has a wire fence, which is child's play for the sheep.

Bethany is a city girl, as she **THE RURAL MINISTER** tells her parishioners. Although always a churchgoer she found her vocation only after seven years in local government, when her career in transport strategy arrived at a crossroads. She has turned that moment into a 'sermonette' – her jolly word – for the Bible Class: 'Sometimes you can't see the road for the traffic. I spent so much time analysing traffic flows and one-way systems that I didn't realise I was stuck in a spiritual tailback. But then the lights turned green and I found myself on the Road to Damascus.'

She served her apprenticeship in a pulpit in the East end of Glasgow, held sleep-overs for the homeless, fasted for the hungry, mounted vigils for world peace. In the days when she ladled soup or organised transport for prisoners' families she could feel that in tiny, tangible ways she was Making a

Difference. Now, as she steps on to the island ferry for the queasy crossing to Nocht, she wonders if her call to the West Highland seaboard has been one of the Almighty's administrative errors.

'Three services each Sunday, a funeral every other week and I'm still not giving them what they want,' she confides ruefully to Father McNeil, the priest at Glenpibroch. 'I took my guitar over to Nocht the other day, thinking at least the Sunday School would enjoy a few verses of One More Step Along the World We Go, but when I turned to pick it up it had disappeared. The session clerk told me later he had 'chust tidied it away'.'

Father McNeil is a sympathetic listener (unlike smug Dr Walpole, whose Episcopalian congregation is small in number but socially conspicuous) but finds it impossible to offer advice without bringing out the Talisker and a spot of emotional blackmail. 'Now, now, lassie, you must keep an old man company, I won't drink alone.' Bethany doesn't want to go down that road. The dram culture has done enough damage in these parts, and the reluctance of her parishioners to seek pastoral counselling is one of her frustrations.

Then there is the driving. She spends more time in her little Ka than she ever spent in urban traffic jams; not only commuting between her three Sunday services but when the kirk session convenes in Dunmachar the round trip is 53 miles. She dreads her first winter. Glenpiproch and Dunmachar have thick walls and central heating but Nocht kirk is a Nissen hut. 'Get a dram inside ye before the service, lassie,' recommends Father McNeil.

As Bethany steps ashore there's a hint of early snow in the wind but her escort of Elders is coatless, although the meaty nose of Donald John MacDonald is red with cold. 'As agreed, Minister,' he reminds her, 'we're expecting a longer sermon this Sunday. And don't worry, we'll make sure they won't fall asleep.'

To Bethany's relief the heaters have been turned on. But when she produces the notes for her sermon ('Do your sheep and chickens have souls?') Donald John rises and turns them off. As the temperature drops she thinks wistfully of the consoling fug in her East End church.

Grant has just bought a handheld GPS. 'Global Positioning System,' he briskly explains to Stewart, his elderly colleague and walking companion. Stewart has taken 12 years to complete all 284 Munros and is now on his second circuit. Grant plans to do them in five. He believes Stewart's tardiness is down to his dependence on time-consuming anachronisms like compass and map and his tedious habit of pausing to admire views or look at birds.

With fake modesty Grant calls himself a health worker. A consultant cardio-thoracic surgeon, he has come late to Sir Hugh Munro's much revised Tables, but expects to hack them by the time he's 50. To this end he **THE MUNROBAGGER** subscribes to the magazine *The Great Outdoors*, he is on Rohan's catalogue mailing list and he has an account at Tiso. There is nothing he doesn't know about advanced insole systems, ergonomic expedition solutions or anything by North Face.

Grant has gone from fair-weather rambler to serious hillwalker in nine months. His navigational skills are sketchy and he has relied on Stewart's experience for his first 41 tops, none of which has been 'technically challenging', as the book puts it. He has been slightly startled, however, by some of the advice in the Scottish Mountaineering Club's Munro guide, and

is wary of adjectives like 'exposed' or 'sporting' when used in connection with ridge walks or summit scrambles.

But in Stewart's company he always pushes for the whole package: not just Beinn Alligan but its Horns, too; not just the Cluanie Ridge but all seven tops; not just An Teallach but its four 'airy' towers. He has also become a wilderness polemicist, holding strong views on cairns as waymarks ('They defile the landscape, in my opinion – I've kicked a few into oblivion') and the siting of bothies. He has yet to stay in a bothy and privately dreads the remote Letterewe and Fisherfield Munros, where an overnight in Shenavall bothy is almost mandatory if he wants to scoop all six.

Grant prefers to celebrate his triumphs with dinner in the nearest country house hotel, where he is often joined by his wife. ('Angela's not much for the Great Outdoors, but she enjoys helping me write up my log book.') If he is to meet his target he must average 1.9 Munros a week and tackle all-weather walking. Hence his current research into thermal gloves and the new GPS. Stewart has cautioned him against the gismo without the back-up of a compass, but Grant is about to dump his companion. He tells Angela, 'I'm not wasting any more time looking for sodding dotterels.'

And so he finds himself alone on a fine spring day on

Craig Meagaidh, which, with its complex topography and precipitous corries, is an ambitious choice for a solo walker of limited experience. But Grant is well-prepared. He has spent several weeks mastering the technology of the GPS, he has a new pair of North Face Sidecut sunglasses, and his daybag is stocked with high-energy snacks and Red Bull. Besides, his 'base camp' near Loch Laggan has been short-listed for Hotel of the Year.

The cloud comes down as Grant is retracing his steps from the summit, where he has called Angela on his mobile to report that he's beaten the SMC estimate by 20 minutes. Soon he is walking blind over scree where the cairns have been kicked into oblivion by some wilderness zealot. Time to consult the Follow Me programme on his GPS.

The little VDU flickers briefly into life before becoming opaque; much like Grant's view beyond two metres of scree slope. 'Crap battery,' he mutters, after five minutes' thumbing of buttons. He is beginning to feel lonely. Somewhere in the stubborn cloud he hears birds twittering and thinks, with a mixture of regret and resentment, 'bloody Stewart would know what they are. And where we are.'

Bunty is the second cousin of the Earl's stepsister, and has a grace-and-favour cottage on the estate. In her darker moments she asks herself who is doing whom the favour, as the cottage has been spurned by every employee from the head keeper to the gardener's apprentice, and Bunty is required to meet its maintenance costs from her meagre salary.

Until defeated by the installation of a computer, (and replaced by a pert young thing with a diamanté stud in her nose and glitter polish on her keyboard-savvy fingernails) she was the factor's secretary, but now guides tourists round selected rooms of the country seat of one of Scotland's noble families.

'Wasted on most of them,' she informs Alexandra, her closest friend, who runs courses in decoupage in the village. 'Your average day tripper from the Central **THE TOUR GUIDE** Belt thinks Chippendale chairs come in flatpacks from Ikea. But I do my best to open their eyes to the rare craftsmanship of our treasures.'

Bunty is not entirely happy in her work. The factor insists she wears a kind of uniform – full skirt and fitted waist-coat in the clan tartan – and it doesn't suit her figure, which is a touch top-heavy. But she does take satisfaction in exercising the authority of an 'honorary chatelaine', as she puts it.

She is gracious to the independent visitor, who is generally respectful of the parking arrangements and occasionally mistakes her for the Earl's mother, but coach parties require watching. The drivers have been known to maul the verges of the Regent's Lawn and deposit cigarette ends in the Etruscan urns, and the behaviour of their passengers is often unpredictable.

'The other day,' she tells Alexandra over their Friday G and T, 'I caught one old dear in the dining room ducking under the ropes to flick the tableware with her thumb. She had the cheek to say she wanted to know if the wine glasses were real crystal. And her friend asked if we sold any paintings in the gift shop like the Veronese in the dining room! You wouldn't believe the ignorance...'

Bunty's pet hates, however, are the visitors who are anything but ignorant, but who have dedicated the years of their retirement to collecting stately homes 'in a most competitive way,' as she complains. 'You name it, they've been there, every noble house in the country from Longleat to the Castle of Mey. They can be very condescending about OUR place, demanding to know why we don't have any Gainsboroughs or Gobelins tapestries.'

Shortly after Easter her patience is put to the test.

With heavy heart and forced smile she welcomes a group from the specialist tour company Big House Buffs. They have their own guide. William's long silver hair is contained by a ponytail and he wastes no time in letting her know he has first class honours in Fine Art from St Andrews.

Two minutes into their tour and Bunty's function is reduced to opening doors and pointing. When she tries to say a few words about moulded ceilings William interrupts with a seminar on Italian plasterwork. When she confuses the periods of the painters Raeburn and Ramsay he crisply corrects her, causing her cheeks to burn and her heart to flood with fury.

Still flustered, she invites him to take the lead into the ill-lit wine cellar and – after a moment's reflection – issues the usual warning to count the steps. 'There are ten,' she advises, as he marches downstairs. 'Or is it nine...?'

Too late. The X-ray of William's ankle requires a round trip of 102 miles, but the Big House Buffs have one consolation: Bunty completes their tour.

Eilidh's Grand Cherokee has two stickers in the rear window: 61
Baby on Board and Breast is Best. She would like to promote
the fact that she's also a Friend of Loch Lomond, but a third
sticker might compromise her rear view. Anyway, she doesn't
have time these days to be friendly to the Bonnie Banks.
She had her first baby five months ago and – as she tells her
former colleagues at Events Solutions – 'he's quite a career move!'

 For a few weeks after Ben's birth, panicked into rigorous,
housebound feeding schedules, Eilidh missed the workplace.
Now she feels liberated. She has made the decision to be a full-
time mum, and the National Childbirth Trust, through its
ante-natal preparation classes and post-natal coffee mornings,
has supplied her with a coterie of kindred spirits. Her
accountant husband was grudging in his approval. 'I suppose
you expect me to keep up your pension contributions, too,'
Mark had grumbled, complaining in the same breath that all
the fun had gone out of accounting.

 She never feels isolated, as she **THE YUMMY MUMMY**
has heard some mothers complain. Responding to the
instructions in The New Contented Little Baby Book ('You
must fit in at least five feeds before midnight to avoid more
than one waking in the night') she has started breastfeeding in
public. Her zeal borders on exhibitionism, and she has trained

herself to ignore the furtive leers of male students in the coffee houses of Byers Road, where she and her new friends exchange tips, gossip and anecdotes behind blockades of buggies, oblivious to the awkward manoeuvres and exasperation of the servers.

She has discovered there is more to motherhood than changing nappies and rocking cradles. 'It's a whole new culture!' she enthuses to her former PA, who drooled obediently over Ben's first presentation but now gets a little tight-lipped when he is pushed into the office during her brief, deskbound lunch hours. 'I wouldn't know,' Sheila responds tartly. 'By the time I pick up Lynsey from school and Lauren from the minder I'm all cultured out.'

Eilidh, however, is a member of Bugaboo Joggers, which allows her to keep fit while propelling Ben at five mph along the walkways of Kelvinside. 'Gangway – Baby Express,' she calls cheerily to the dithering dog-walkers as they scatter before the lightweight Bugaboo pram, envy of idler mums. She also takes a class in Brain Games for Babies and Toddlers and has put down her name for a seminar in sign language. ('No, Mark, there's nothing wrong with Ben's hearing but baby signing allows me to communicate with him before he learns to speak.') And today she is on her way from the rugged hinterland of Glasgow, where the only off-road driving she does is into her Bearsden car port, to a new mother-and-baby yoga class at a West End fitness centre.

'Shit – sorry, Ben.' A middle-aged woman in a Skoda Fabia has beaten her into the last dedicated parking space for Parent and Child. Eilidh has seen this woman before. She has no baby, no toddler, no car seat – nothing to indicate she's entitled to occupy this space. Time to confront her. 'Excuse me.' Eilidh looks down at her from the fortified heights of the Cherokee. 'Are you aware these bays are reserved for Parent and Child?'

The woman smiles pleasantly as she walks towards the gym. 'That's all right,' she calls over her shoulder. 'I am a Parent and I've got a Child. She's 23 now. If you can't manage to carry your baby for an extra few metres then you really ought to do some work on your upper body strength.'

Eilidh, unusually, is lost for words.

Kirsty is Douglas's Flower of Scotland. She is first on her feet when the 15 warriors storm onto the field to fight another battle for the Calcutta Cup. Be it Murrayfield or Twickenham, no chest swells more conspicuously than the billowy bosom of Kirsty's rugby shirt; no voice soars more piercingly than the upper register of her soprano. Douglas is proud of her passion, and squeezes her hand on each thunderous syllable of 'be a nay-shun ah-gen.'

Douglas was still playing prop forward for Tweedside Academicals when they met. Kirsty had been co-opted into a party of support for their opponents, her college team, and spent the first half of the match giggling over the rumpus of the ruck. She had never seen a match before, not even on television, and cast herself in the role of social anthropologist: 'If you saw this nonsense taking place in a remote clearing in the Borneo rainforest you would think you had discovered some primitive religious ritual. Bottom-worship, perhaps.'

Yet there was something about Douglas's bottom, not to mention his straining thighs, which mesmerised her. She found herself quizzing her male companions on the rules of the game, then standing on tiptoe for every scrum. 'Is it true they all take baths together? And flick each other **THE RUGBY FANS** with wet towels? I'd like to be a fly-half on the wall for that spectacle!'

Tweedside Academicals won the day and Kirsty contrived to be standing at the bar when the victors exploded into the Reiver's Return. Douglas had never met a woman who was keen to stand the first round, and by the time he'd sunk his fifth pint of Tup's Heavy he had lost his heart. They were married 18 months later. Kirsty carried a bouquet shaped like a rugby ball. When she tossed it over her shoulder it was kicked into touch – the marquee – by Tweedside's star full back. The caterers tried to smile over the tray of glasses dropped by a startled waitress.

Looking back, Kirsty and Douglas judged this incident 'innocent fun'. Not a bit like the behaviour that afflicts the game today. When they first went to internationals together the car park at Murrayfield was a civilised venue for pre-match lunches with friends. Kirsty packed the hamper with hearty picnics: Henderson's wholemeal bread, home-made quiche and individual tureens of her own pâté (chicken liver – no such thing as a vegetarian option in those days) while Douglas provided bottles of Cockburn's claret.

Their fellow supporters were Borders farmers or professionals: solid family lawyers, tweedy GPs, mill managers. All had wives who preferred to be elsewhere, but Kirsty was soon able to read a game as knowledgeably as the men. Those

68

were the glory days of Andy Irvine and John Jeffrey; but when Scotland began bidding for the Wooden Spoon it was no coincidence, in her opinion, that the character of the crowd deteriorated with the performance of the national side.

'We've given up our car park lunches,' she now tells friends. 'Too many yobs at Murrayfield these days. You'd think the Calcutta Cup was a football international. And as for those corporate spivs boozing in their boxes – whatever happened to serious commitment?'

When the Five Nations Championship becomes the Six Nations Championship Kirsty's passion is rekindled. The Italians, although rarely successful, bring new glamour to the game, and she and Douglas take to week-ending in Rome when Italy play Scotland at home. At the start of the new season, however, Douglas turns up alone, looking glum. 'Kirsty's moved to Italy,' he explains sourly to the old gang. 'She's living with a 24-year-old full back from Pisa.'

Adrian has always wanted to own a distillery. Single malt, of **69**
course. Preferably an island one, with a waterfront site of
exquisite loveliness. When a friend in **THE WHITE SETTLER**
the City tells him that Ghillebuidhe has ceased production and
its plant on Eilean Ceannmor has been mothballed by its
Japanese owners, he sees an opportunity. Eilean Ceannmor is
hard to reach – two flights and a ferry – but before his partner
can say, 'Where's the nearest Waitrose?' he is checking into The
Exciseman for a recce.

Two hours later, nursing a large Ghillebuidhe ('the
last of the 16-year-old Distiller's Edition,' the barman mentions)
Adrian realises his pipedream has gone up in smoke. The
distillery is not only mothballed but cobwebbed, crumbling onto
a drab shoreline near the new sewage plant. The stock is down
to its last five casks. No City consortium would look at such an
iffy investment, 'so no golden-haired laddie for me,' he tells
himself morosely, having taken the trouble to get the English
translation for Ghillebuidhe.

But before he leaves the island he has an epiphany.
He takes an early morning walk to the shell-sand beach and
feels the great bright space around him fill his soul. He hears a
glad cry overhead and sees a mighty skein of geese heading
south to their feeding grounds on the farmers' fields of Islay.

One squadron of geese banks out of the formation and glides down to land just a few yards from Adrian's seat on the machair.

Back in Highgate, he explains to Justin: 'I felt they were telling me I'd come home.'

Six months later, as the barnacle geese prepare to return to Greenland, Adrian and Justin open an antiquarian bookshop and tea-room in the old Ghillebuidhe visitor centre. 'Got the premises on a peppercorn lease,' Adrian tells his London friends, 'but our wee hoose was a different matter. Every third cottage in the village is a second home and we needed all the capital from the Highgate flat to buy our place and do it up.'

Adrian and Justin are sensitive to local issues. There are 26 committees on the island (one for every 60-odd people) and in no time at all they are members of the Bothy Preservation Society, the Uisgebeatha Connoisseurs Club and the Eilean Ceannmor Mole Conservation Trust which, despite opposition from farmers, seeks to protect the indigenous species of mole. They are surprised to discover the office-bearers are mainly immigrants from the mainland, but when Adrian is elected to the community council he gets his first taste of native authority.

The chairperson is Heather-Belle MacLean, whose family has had the home farm since 1831, although she's always careful to explain that her ancestors had nothing to do with the Laird's agricultural reforms. A large, boisterous woman who breeds Clydesdales (and has failed to persuade her ploughman to use them for turning the barley fields) she often chairs meetings in her dungarees.

When Adrian uses his 'maiden' speech to describe how the Highgate Interaction Network could be a model for improving communications between the island's activists and their local authority, Heather-Belle is gracious. 'I'm sure we can learn from your experience, Adrian, as you can from ours. You do know how Eilean Ceannmor got its name, don't you? It means 'island of the big head', and it was a big-headed chap from Islay who came here yonks ago with a view to taking charge.'

'They say it was his body the archeologists from Historic Scotland found in the Glas peat hag. Well preserved and pretty much intact, apart from his big head.'

Charlotte's first choice was St Andrews, despite the fact that **73** Prince William has gone. Although she claims to be Scottish 'on Daddy's side' she has only twice visited Scotland; once when her parents toyed with the idea of buying a shooting lodge in Wester Ross, once when the Upper Sixth took *The Prime of Miss Jean Brodie* to Edinburgh's Festival Fringe. **THE YOONI YAH** When she filled in her UCAS form she imagined St Andrews was on Edinburgh's doorstep, giving her access to style bars, George Street clubs and Harvey Nichols, but was alarmed to discover the old university town is marooned on a windswept North Sea coast. So she plumped for the capital itself.

Charlotte is a city girl. 'Holland Park, actually,' she tells the concierge, as the porters are now called, when she tours the university halls of residence. The man looks confused: 'Ye don't sound foreign,' he remarks. 'Ah've only ever been to Holland once, on ma mate's stag, and Ah canny remember much aboot it. Is Holland Park anywhere near Amsterdam?'

Her squeal of laughter makes the concierge wince. 'I'm not Dutch! I come from HOLLAND PARK – you know – Holland Park in London.'

A year into her degree course (Balkan Ceramic Art and Sanskrit) Charlotte leaves Pollock Halls for her own double upper flat overlooking the Meadows, which she shares with two

sisters from Bath and the son of a Nigerian diplomat. 'You know what Daddy's like with his investment portfolio,' she moans lightly to friends. 'He insisted on buying into Edinburgh.' She is unfailingly polite to her Marchmont neighbours when they complain of late-night noise – 'I'm afraid Jonas and his band were rehearsing for a very important gig' – and her apologies couldn't be more charmingly offered.

She has no way of knowing that the high pitch of her voice and the cutting edge of her vowels are enough to trigger prejudice in her neighbours' bosoms – not to mention an ancient, atavistic hostility in their very viscera; just as she has no way of knowing that their commiseration, when England's Test team runs into trouble on the cricket grounds of the Punjab, is insincere.

Charlotte feels she has integrated well in Edinburgh. The bar staff at the Opal Lounge call her Charlie and tell her she looks like Sienna Miller, and she has achieved modest celebrity among the student population for the lavish catering at her supper parties. 'I try to buy locally,' she tells guests. 'Cheese from Ian Mellis and Aberdeen Angus fillet burgers from The Store. But Mummy seems to think we live on haggis up here, so she keeps sending me hampers from Fortnum and Mason.'

The city's fashion quarter, Multrees Walk, is like a

mini Knightsbridge and Charlotte and her circle of girlfriends find that Edinburgh's retail industry can meet their seasonal needs. On nights out she is effortlessly stylish in Ugg boots, big belt and ra-ra skirt, her Whistles top accessorised with an eclectic mix of jewellery: chunky Tiffany necklace, Gucci watch and some ethnic bits and pieces picked up on her gap year, for which her father provided a round-the-world ticket.

As she unknots her pashmina ('the genuine article – got it in Katmandu') and opens her new Chloé Betty bag she pushes to the back of her mind the unfinished essay on Montenegro's glazing traditions. It is student night at Why Not and the bar is loud with belly laughs and high octane banter. She feels at home. Why, after two or three vodkas with Millie, Arthur and Sam it's easy to forget she's in Scotland.

August in Glen Dour has never been quite the same since Silkie Slingback bought the Castle. As tradition requires, the new chatelaine has become honorary chieftain of the Highland Games, a role she enthusiastically fulfils 'in tribute to my roots.' Silkie's Gaelic lineage can be traced back to the Barras Ballroom in Glasgow and a certain night in 1951, when her father, fresh from the Isles, fell into the company of an apprentice manicurist from Maryhill. Nine months later, when the Hebridean Lothario was **THE CELEBRITY CHIEFTAIN** presented with his daughter, he declared she looked like 'a wee seal pup' and called her Silkie.

Her surname, inspired by her signature shoes, came later, when she acquired an agent with a taste for alliteration and went solo. She had outgrown the Fair Isle sweaters and bearded strummers of the Luckenpennies, whose repertoire was bogged down in Celtic Folk, and cut her first hit single with a rock ballad called Blue Collar Blondie. From then on, Silkie never looked back. In the 1970s she was seldom out of the charts; in the 80s she began writing songs with a political edge (who can forget *Hit Me With Your Handbag, Maggie?*) and in the 90s she did several international tours with the boy band Platinum Zits.

Marriages came and went, but she has now found

happiness with a Platinum Zit, despite the age gap. They don't often visit their Highland home; Zak is planning a revival tour of the Zits and Silkie is now a chat show host on daytime TV. But they never miss the Games. Zak wears his black kilt with silver pinstripe and Silkie's tartan slingbacks are teamed with something ethnic by Stella McCartney or tartan by Vivienne Westwood. What's more, their house guests are household names from show business, television and occasionally politics. (Silkie's friend Scarlett was once mistaken for Cherie Blair).

Among local opinion there are two camps: rubber-neckers and reactionaries. The rubber-neckers argue that Silkie's Highland Games put Glen Dour on the media map, which is good for tourism. The reactionaries lament the passing of the old Laird and the Way Things Were: mild-mannered Sir Tavish in his drooping kilt and MCC tie, the WRI in charge of catering, the wee Highland dancers rehearsing their steps behind the marquee. And the weather was always reliably wet, whereas it hasn't rained once since Silkie became chieftain. Somehow she even manages to book the climate for what she calls 'my favourite gig'.

She has also taken command of the catering; tea and bacon rolls have been replaced by smoothies and sushi, the bar groans under buckets of Pol Roger and after her first warm G and T Silkie donated an ice-making machine. The schoolgirl dancers trip over their swords as they crane their necks to spot the celebrities, and there is now a helipad on the clearing once reserved for the solo piping event.

On the day itself, the chieftain's chopper is secured to the ground with guy ropes, but a capricious West wind tugging at the blades puts a gleam in Hector's eye. Hector the Heavy, triple champion of hammer, shot and caber, is not one of Silkie's fans. 'A tricky day for the hammer,' he mentions to Zak, who has been spraying him with champagne. 'These gusts are strong enough to affect the throw.'

Prophetic words. The champion's most prodigious birl sends the hammer wildly off-course, over the crowd and into the helicopter cockpit. 'It's a mercy only yon wee whirlybird got hurt,' says Hector, with a sly smile.

Standing glum-faced in the garden of her home Griselda Mackenzie stares at a planter of geraniums. 'You shouldn't be blooming,' she tells them crossly. 'You should be dying of frostbite!' She sighs and gazes past the opulent sandstone villas of King's Park towards the Trossachs, which remain stubbornly green. Even the bracken is late in turning. Below the hills she can just glimpse the sparkle of the Lake of Menteith. 'Nineteen seventy-nine,' she mutters to Brueghel the Elder. 'Do you think I'll live to see another Bonspiel on the lake, old chap?' The greyhound pushes his sharp, aristocratic nose into her hand and gives a sympathetic whine.

Griselda's mother put her foot

THE CURLING SKIP

down when her father wanted to call her Grizel – 'a fine old Scots name' – although the compromise wasn't a happy one. At school and then college it inspired nicknames like Grisly or (when she was going through her Afghan coat phase) Grizzly Bear. But since she became the respected skip of Team Mackenzie she has come to value her name and enjoys seeing it in print, where it looks not only dignified but heroic. Indeed, practising for the European Play Downs, she has privately rolled the title 'Griselda Mackenzie MBE' round her tongue.

Now that it is officially a Winter Olympics sport (and most especially since the gold medal triumph of Team

Scotland) the media profile of the roaring game has never been higher. As she tells her cousin Heather, who is visiting from New Zealand, 'I no longer need a magnifying glass to find out how we did at the Kilmacolm Aurora Borealis Refrigerator Curlathon. And that wee bauchle who freelances for the Advertiser wants a quote about our chances of qualifying for Basel.'

To her enduring regret Griselda has never played outdoors. She was only 18 in 1979, when the last Bonspiel was held on the Lake of Menteith, and in those days she thought curling had something to do with the housekeeping of skating rinks. Today, as her few non-curling friends will testify (usually rolling their eyes) there is nothing she can't tell them about its history, traditions, rules, tactics and science. 'Friction is all!' is her discreet but inspiring battle cry when she concludes her team talk on the eve of important tournaments.

She has even named her dog, latest in a dynasty of greyhounds, after the celebrated Dutch artist who painted peasants sliding rocks across a frozen pond – the first known picture of a game of curling. 'But it was us Scots who invented it,' she reminds overseas visitors. 'There's a reference to curling in the records of Paisley Abbey for 1541. And you'll never find a better stone than Ailsa Craig granite.'

Heather has been so infected by Griselda's enthusiasm that she has taken up the sport herself in distant Dunedin. But she is currently at risk of losing patience with her cousin's obsession with climate change. 'Get over yourself, Grisly,' she tells her tartly. 'You talk as though the desertification of Africa and the swamping of the Maldives are petty inconveniences compared with the disaster of an ice-free Lake of Menteith. It's only a game, indoors or outside.'

When she receives an email from Dunedin, however, she becomes a little furtive. Griselda surprises her on the phone to Air New Zealand. 'Change of plan,' she explains awkwardly. 'I've got to get home as soon as possible. There's been a freak cold snap in the Southern Alps and one of the lakes is frozen. Every major club in South Island is heading for the Bonspiel.'

There is only one word for Griselda's expression: frosty.

The late Ringan Macnab, head ghillie on the finest salmon beat
north of the Spey, was a devotee of Scottish literature. When
his first son was born he called him John, in homage to the
collective *nom de guerre* of the gentleman-poachers of the John
Buchan novels. The real John Macnab is to carry the legacy of
his name into an age when Buchan's books are rarely read and
there are (in his opinion) few proper sportsmen left on the
river. 'Nothin' but jumped-up barrow boys whose idea o'
comedy is takin' the mick oot o' ma accent,' he grumbles.

This is not entirely true. The Laird can still put
together a fishing party of some quality: men and women who
wear their noble lineage modestly and show decent reverence
for the ghillie's rivercraft, even if they are prone to slap their
empty pockets for forgotten cheque books and pour him hefty
drams of the Laird's malt in lieu of **THE GRUMPY GHILLIE**
tips. 'The true toffs are aye tight-fisted,' he opines indulgently.
'It's how they hang on to their big hooses.'

As a young man he was reluctant to follow his father's
calling and spent some years in Bo'ness, working for the
Conservative Party as agent to the local candidate. His man
lost his deposit in three General Elections but the job did give
Macnab the opportunity to meet Harold Macmillan, the former
Prime Minister, as he toured West Lothian in an effort to rouse

the Tory faithful. When Macnab mentioned his father had once ghillied for him the Elder Statesman slapped his back. 'John Macnab! With a name like that you should be up to your thighs in peat-brown water, not up to your neck in lost causes.'

The advice was taken. Four decades later Macnab knows every swirl and eddy in the River Thrift. He has adapted, grudgingly, to the forces of commerce. When not escorting the Laird's private guests he is guiding 'new money' – corporate lawyers, IT consultants and night club entrepreneurs with £300 wading jackets and state-of-the-art platinum rods. The ghillie calls them 'angling tourists', his mood rarely improved by their anecdotes about bone fishing in the Bahamas, trout fishing in Chile or blue water fishing off the Seychelles.

There is pressure from the Laird to give them good sport. 'Hard times, John. If we can up the catch statistics we can up next season's rents. Don't let them waste time on lunch.' And so the reputation of John Macnab becomes admired, feared and mocked at fishing camps round the globe. One of his regulars, a retired professional footballer called Stevie Gough, calls him 'the Alex Ferguson of the piscatorial world' and pretends to forget his name. 'Fergie, isn't it? What kind of water torture have you got for me today?'

Macnab simmers; takes his client the long way round,

by way of spongy peat and knee-high heather, to the Sprachle Pool and makes him move upriver on every third cast. 'Give us a break, Fergie,' moans Stevie Gough, after six hours of fruitless casting in a bitter drizzle. 'If this were the Zambezi my basket would be full of tiger fish and I'd be on my second sundowner. Call this fishing?'

'Aye weel,' says Macnab, who has chosen to ignore the Laird's instructions. 'It's the River Thrift, nae the Zambezi, and if ye canny land the King o' Fish ye canny call yersel' a fly fisherman.' The sour smile he permits himself is worth forfeiting the wad of notes which is Stevie's usual tip.

Broch Basketry is a dreich place in November. The last leaves have been stripped from the birches, and Megan misses their glow. She's happy to boast to visitors that the cottage water supply comes straight off the hill, but after 10 days of rain the noise from the burn and its waterfalls is almost insufferable. 'Like living with the constant flushing of a giant loo,' she moans, conscious that the complaint bemuses her sister, who sentimentally applauds every tweet, rustle and gurgle of the natural world.

Kirsty has just arrived from Glasgow, but neither Megan nor Strathboorach are at their most tranquil in autumn. Jumpy pheasants cackle alarm calls, distraught ewes seek their abattoir-bound lambs, and the stags are rutting. Even after nine years in the strath Megan hasn't got used to their territorial bellows, which to her urban ears sound like the collective groan of a football crowd whose team has just missed a winning goal in the dying seconds of a cup final. 'What do you have to do to get a bit of peace and quiet **THE COUNTRY CRAFTSWOMAN** around here?' she grumbles, as she lugs a bundle of split Cumbrian oak and a fat bolt of willow from the shed to the kitchen. She is behind schedule with her Christmas orders, and her numb fingers struggle with the bindings. The power is down.

It was a dry stane dyker called Garth who lured Megan

to the Northern Highlands with the promise of a simpler, quieter, stress-free life. She was teaching art in a sink school in Renfrewshire, and when she saw the cottage by the broch the needs of her pupils were consigned to history. After two months Garth left her for an extreme sports instructor, offering his tenancy of the cottage by way of apology along with several unpaid bills. But it was still summer, there were tourists around and Megan detected a niche market. The nearest crafts outlet – an unimaginative pottery – was over 30 miles away, so she decided to turn her hobby of basketmaking into an income.

She's had some success. She keeps in touch with new techniques through the summer schools of the Basketmakers' Association and has even planted her own small holt of willow. The bread and butter of her passing trade are wine baskets and trugs, shoppers and pet carriers, but her most creative work is reserved for the mail order brochure, which features her customised version of the Orkney chair (its back is interwoven with mosses, teazles and baby catkins) and a very superior cradle, which is an ambitious adaptation of her Cumbrian oak swills. Three chairs and two cradles are on order for Christmas, and Kirsty's visit is not timely. Her sister takes little interest in her craft, but occasionally uses the premises of Broch Basketry as her 'layby in the fast lane of telemarketing', as she puts it.

'I'm going to lock up the hens,' Megan tells her unwelcome sibling, who is holding out blue hands to the embers in the wood-burning stove. 'That's the last of the logs, but the power will be back soon.' When she returns to the cottage she finds Kirsty, looking pleased with herself, warming her backside by the stove, which is roaring cheerfully. 'I found a pile of sticks and twigs and things in the kitchen so I flung them in. They make a good blaze, don't they?'

The basketmaker, transfixed, watches weeks of work – the soaked, boiled, split and mellowed makings of her five most profitable Christmas orders – go up in smoke.

Mungo Laird was introduced to whisky with his mother's milk.
Literally. Lady Laird belonged to the dram culture of her class,
which morphed into gentry from trade somewhere around
1880. (The product which made the family fortune was Laird's
Relief: 'Keeping the Empire Regular'. Samples of its
advertisements, showing beaming sepoys digging latrines in
the Hindu Kush, are sometimes included in exhibitions of
Victorian graphics). When breast-feeding the infant Mungo 'in
the glory days before the quacks and killjoys took the fun out of
maternity' his mother saw no reason to alter her habits. 'Two
fingers of Glenswally before dinner, three fingers after, and the
son and heir sleeps like a top!'

Fifty-six years later, Mungo still sleeps like a top; for
at least three hours, before heartburn sets in. 'Freedom,
Whisky and Rennies gang thegither!' is his jocose response to
the price paid for a pleasure which is also a duty. He is a
leading light of Uisgebeatha Envoys, an association dedicated
to the celebration of the classic malts while fund-raising for the
Society of Indigenous Maltmen. His mother, now a fiery
octogenarian, still cracks the whip over the **THE WHISKY BORE**
staff at the racing stables, leaving him plenty of time to refine
his passion for the amber liquid.

It is Mungo's current role to organise charity tastings,

and when he proposes the stables as a venue for the next event
Lady Laird is unenthusiastic. She loves drinking the stuff, but
has no interest in Mungo's expertise and can barely distinguish
a Lowland malt from a luxury blend. However, the thought of
so much whisky swilling around the cup room is irresistible.
'Just don't ask me to spit it out and talk nonsense about the
flavour. Whisky tastes like whisky to me, not blaeberries
scorched over a fire of Scots pine on a South Uist beach.'

Mungo is excited. The event is competitive and he has
invited the country's most distinguished connoisseurs, who will
taste 10 single malts and be required to identify the year of the
bottling, the provenance of the barley and the pot stills, the
name of the maltman's grandfather and the gender of the
distillery cat. He himself will take part, but only after everyone
else has confided their results to notepads. His mother has
agreed to charge the glasses and her head groom has been
tasked with selecting and researching the malts so that
Mungo's tasting is as blind as those of his competitors.

Mungo is over-excited. While his guests work their
way through their ten samples he has a stiff snifter or three of
Moine Musgach from his hip flask. He is soothed by its familiar
flavour, which he calls 'a subtle fusion of heather honey, fresh
herring, second-day broth and – dare I say it? – the liquid

version of Lairds' Relief.' There is nothing anyone can tell him about his favourite malt.

All the same, his palate isn't as clean as it might be when he steps forward to take his turn; which may be why every measure of whisky tastes identical. In growing confusion he snatches and re-snatches glasses, gulps their contents and drops his empty notepad before proclaiming desperately, 'Moine Musgach, 1991. The barley comes from Glaur Farm, the stills were made in Rothes, the maltman's grandfather was Archie Thrapple and the cat is a ginger tom.'

'Wrong!' barks Lady Laird, with a wink at his guests. 'It's Tiger's Milk, 2003. The barley comes from the Punjab, the stills were made in Mumbai, the maltman's grandfather was Rajan Singh and the cat got eaten by a jackal.'

Loudon and Sue acquired their market garden in Angus five years ago. 'A smallholding, actually,' Sue tells people, by way of drawing attention to the presence of the Krankies (their three goats) and an equally cantankerous stock of assorted hens. Their combined experience – Loudon was a horticultural researcher and Sue a home economics teacher – gave the impetus to an idea which began, like so many dreams, on a Mediterranean holiday.

'I have the soul of a peasant,' Sue claims. 'In another life I truly believe I came from a family of *contadini*.' Once, on the obscure Greek island which she and Loudon found by 'sticking a pin in the ferry timetable', she offered to help with the olive harvest. The bemused farmer handed her a basket and pointed to a ladder. After 20 minutes under the sun and among the branches of a venerable tree she climbed down, pleading vertigo. To make amends she bought two kilos of olives, further puzzling the farmer with her efforts to explain, in pidgin Greek, that she was more of a Scottish peasant.

Loudon sensibly confined his interest in micro food production to the local markets, with their cornucopias of fresh comestibles, and his account of how they had inspired their own **THE FARMERS' MARKET STALLHOLDER** enterprise always includes the jocose punchline, 'and that's

where the seed was planted.' Their city-born twins, now cynical 13-year-olds, roll their eyes and turn up the volume of their MP3 players. The twins' support on farmers' market Saturdays is only enlisted with bribes: a trip to the Cineplex in Dundee, or The Killers' latest CD.

Loudon and Sue grow rare varieties of potato, organic soft fruits and tomatoes in polytunnels. ('Seasonality is sacred to us, but we've got to make some compromises to keep us going throughout the year'). It is one of Sue's tasks to transform some of their strawberries, raspberries and blackcurrants into jams made to her own recipes. Her range of 'compotes' is called Bonjour Grand-mère, which leads to some confusion at her market stall. 'French then, are they?' customers often ask. As she has no intention of changing the name and trashing 2000 tastefully designed labels, Sue has learned to tell smooth little white lies. 'The fruit is our own produce, of course, but the recipes are my grandmother's. She came from Normandy.'

After some perseverance she has fulfilled a cherished ambition. She has secured a spot at Edinburgh farmers' market, reportedly the best in the UK. Awkwardly, the launch of Bonjour Grand-mère at the prestigious site beneath Edinburgh Castle clashes with Loudon's lecture to the Aberdeenshire Slow Food Convivium. (His paper is entitled, 'The Future of the

Tomato: Fruit or Vegetable?') She must engage the co-operation of the twins, and after some negotiation they agree to help set up the stall and serve the elite of the capital's Eco-gastronomic consumers.

It is an exciting morning. Sue is intoxicated by the smell of spit-roasted hog and Arbroath haddies curing in a portable smoker, and despite heavy competition from rare breed pork, ostrich mince, single-brewery beers, venison haggis, speciality cheeses, fruit wines, and any amount of organic vegetables and well-hung beef, Bonjour Grand-mère makes a modest impact.

With only a dozen jars of compote unsold they drive back to Angus, where dusk is falling over the Forfar by-pass and the golden arches of its roadside McDonalds. 'I'll pick you up in half an hour,' Sue hisses at the twins, as they put in their order for double cheeseburgers with extra fries and large Cokes. 'Just try to avoid being seen by anyone we know.'

'Look at this,' says Eleanor distastefully, pointing a finger at a page in her issue of Scotland in Trust. 'Virgin Balloons! It says

THE NATIONAL TRUST FOR SCOTLAND MEMBERS

here the Trust has teamed up with Virgin Balloons to offer 'a new way of seeing Trust properties'. For heaven's sake! What's wrong with the old way?'

Roderick shakes his head in silent solidarity. There are times when he too feels that their long commitment to Scotland's heritage and its custodians is being sorely tested by the pace of change at the NTS. Pop concerts at Crathes Castle. Medieval Weekends at Culzean. 'Friendliest Property' competitions. And now hot-air balloons. Roderick and Eleanor have their own word for these activities: 'inappropriate'.

They have been members of the National Trust for Scotland for over 40 years and, indeed, met on a Trust conservation holiday – one of the first work camps on St Kilda. At the time Roderick was completing his thesis on the history of the Soay sheep and at the youthful age of 27 Eleanor had just been promoted to head teacher (or headmistress, as they called her in those days) of a primary school near Dumfries. On Hirta, the main island of the St Kilda group, they helped repair turf roofs and heaved stones for the drystone dyker. This shared experience cemented a relationship which, though childless, has prospered down the decades with the Trust.

Not only are they leading activists of their local Members' Centre and dedicated volunteers at Threave House but they also make a point of visiting Trust headquarters in Charlotte Square whenever they're in Edinburgh. Eleanor takes the opportunity to debunk the dynamic design initiatives coming out of Gardens these days ('In my opinion you can't beat crazy paving with lavender borders') and Roderick, who became an agricultural buildings adviser after finishing his PhD but can name every bird and mammal on the endangered list of endemic species, gives informal advice to the person in charge of Species Rescue. As veteran supporters they believe they have a right to help shape Trust policy.

They have never missed an AGM. Roderick wears his kilt and Eleanor sometimes treats herself to a new outfit, perhaps a useful two-piece (or 'costume', as she still finds herself calling it) from her favourite clothes shop, Barbours of Dumfries. 'The oldest independent department store in Scotland,' she tells her Trust associates. 'The Barbour family have owned and run it since 1856, although people tend to confuse them with the folk who make those ostentatious waxed jackets – fancy dress for people playing lairds, if you ask me.'

Now that St Kilda has acquired its second World Heritage Site designation the couple wonder if they are fit enough for another conservation holiday. They are not yet too old – the upper age limit is 75 – but Eleanor has high blood pressure and Robert's sciatica sometimes gives him gip. 'Maybe we should settle for another cruise.' Every second year they take to the sea and reclaim friendship with the regulars among the NTS's guest lecturers. They much regret the passing of Magnus Magnusson, who mingled genially with the passengers, 'but the least said about a certain very superior art expert from London the better. Seemed to think we weren't sufficiently cultivated to engage his attention over breakfast.'

Robert, however, has been doing a bit of thinking and has another idea. 'I don't suppose,' he asks nervously, conscious he's risking his wife's scorn, 'you would like to see Falkland Palace from the air? Or the Great Garden at Pitmedden? To be honest, I've always fancied a ride in a hot-air balloon.'

Isobel's mother hasn't set foot in Jenners since the tea-room went self-service. She still lives in Morningside, but sold the villa to buy a flat in sheltered housing. Isobel tries not to brood on her mother's timing; the sale went through just before J.K. Rowling moved into Morningside, adding value and cachet to the suburb. But she can't help being a little waspish about Harry Potter.

THE LADY WHO LUNCHES

'Never read a word,' she tells her oldest friend over lunch in Mangiamo, toying with a slice of flabby, barely-cooked aubergine which the menu calls 'char-grilled'. After all those *agriturismo* holidays in Umbria ('Tuscany is full of German hairdressers these days') she knows how char-grilled vegetables should taste, but is reluctant to complain. Her favourite *trattoria* is an outpost of that distinguished Scots-Italian gastro-dynasty Corelli and Vivaldi, and Isobel is secretly intimidated by their reputation.

As Frances tops up their glasses with Pinot Grigio Isobel checks her friend's face for traces of collagen (perky lips) or botox (clenched cheeks) and admires the new highlights in her hair. 'What would you call that colour? Honey blonde?' The least said about the Prada leather trousers the better; in Isobel's opinion Frances's style is too often inspired by the Anne Robinson school of fashion, whereas her own loyalty to

Jaeger cashmeres and Jane Davidson has never faltered. Both women are 57 but look 10 years younger than their mothers at the same age. They often discuss those composed, conscientious and unspeakably dull lives ('What did they DO all day?') but Isobel is haunted by the suspicion that in an odd, post-modern sort of way she is turning into her mother after all.

She's much busier, of course. Mum married a Writer to the Signet, and was only required to hold an annual sherry party for his most important clients. Isobel's husband is a merchant banker, and she's cooked more networking dinners with choice of puddings – 'my own *tarte au citron* or cinnamon poached pears' – than she cares to recall. Her mother never went to university, whereas Isobel dropped out of Art History to marry Kenneth, in a bit of a rush, during the Summer of Love. ('Must have been that night I sicked up the Pill,' she once confessed to Frances, as they deplored the binge drinking of their student children.)

Her mother merely did two mornings a week for Help the Aged, while Isobel has countless committee commitments to hospice fund-raising. In emergencies, she also staffs a shop in the Borders, for the National Trust for Scotland (she is a Member, after all) and has just signed up for a life painting course. Even so, she is not entirely satisfied with her busy diary.

Has she fulfilled her potential? Has she maximised her talents as a People Person? Has she Given Back?

These and other challenges of the Empty Nester are regularly addressed over lunch, which today is her reward for a hectic morning spent re-stocking her patio planters and paying a brief but exasperating visit to her mother. Mum had hooted when Isabel announced she wanted to train as a grief councillor, and demanded to know how she would squeeze it in 'between that Pilates stuff and all your long lunches.'

'So negative,' Isobel tells Frances. 'Of course, they didn't have grief counselling in her day. When Dad died she just redecorated their bedroom.' As she leafs through her wallet for the right banknotes (they always share the bill) she gives a sudden yelp of dismay. She has spotted a splash of olive oil on the taupe suede of her Ferragamo flatties; that cocky young waiter was clearly careless with his salad mixers when he dressed the salad at the table. 'Do you think if I complain those terrifying Corellis will take something off the bill?'

Despite the blight on the neighbourhood Dougie Bell runs a
clean shop. Crumpled crisp packets and stained beer mats
have no place on the tartan formica of his wee tables or the
spotless surface of the bar. The redundant ashtrays, bright
with the logos of long-vanished independent brewers, are wiped
hourly. 'Canny bring masel' tae get rid o' them,' he tells Alec
and Joseph, who have just finished their morning shift at the
sorting office. 'The pub has a naked look without they ashtrays.
And folk can aye use them for their chewin' gum.'

Dougie is a relic. So, too, is The THE LAST PUBLICAN
New Moby Dick, a family business which relocated from the
waterfront when the original Moby Dick was displaced by
development. 'Abody kens jute jam and journalism,' he
morosely informs new customers (an infrequent presence)
puzzled by the name. 'But naebody remembers Dundee once had
the biggest whaling fleet in the country. Ma granda used tae take
orders for penguins for a wee zoo in Camperdown Park.'

His pub is a plain place, built at a time when there
was little money for stained glass, mahogany or brass. It has
few ornamental flourishes, but there is comfort in the nicotine-
stained ceiling and faded linoleum for a certain kind of customer,
and in extreme winter weather Dougie has been known to light
the coal fire. When his father retired he had plans to refurbish,

but they went no farther than opening up the saloon bar 'to the ladies', putting a pool table in the former lounge bar and mounting framed photographs of whalers on the walls.

Marooned on the edge of a brownfield site with provisional planning permission for a leisure centre, The New Moby Dick briefly attracted the attention of a brewing conglomerate. They were prepared to retain Dougie as licensee and manager, but the price required was too high. A young woman from the group's design team paid him a visit and outlined 'a few ideas'. A maritime theme, she thought, but nothing 'retro'.

'Retro is so last century. I'm thinking camp and contemporary – an underwater feel, a bit jokey, maybe a few references to Pirates of the Caribbean. We could take out the pool table and make the lounge bar the family room, with a tropical fish aquarium to entertain the kiddies.'

At the word 'kiddies' a strange rictus afflicted Dougie's face, affecting to be a smile as he showed the designer the door. 'We dinny do bairns in this pub. We dinny do food, apart from peanuts and crisps, or music or fruit machines or video games. We jist aboot do television, but thon set on the wall is 20 years old and it only gets turned on fur internationals or Scotsport. This pub is fur drinkin'.'

He doesn't regret turning down the brewers' offer. Every since Marie refused to return from a visit to her sister in Queensland (something to do with the skipper of a dive boat) his needs have been modest, and The New Moby Dick meets them all. His evening customers include local women of his own generation; his daytime customers are kindred spirits, ageing shift workers, incapacity pensioners and retired dock-workers with memories of the Tay estuary before the *Discovery* returned to its home port to become a visitor attraction.

Best of all he is his own boss. When an American post-graduate student, well out of his territory in the university Department of Biochemistry, diffidently approaches the bar Dougie does not feel obliged to serve him.

'Canny help ye, son, we've nae clean half-pint glasses. In this pub ye either drink pints or get oot.'